FROM GRANDMA-MA

SABRINA PHILLIPS EVANS

Illustrations by Monmon Akter

From Grandma-Ma

Sabrina Phillips Evans
Illustrations by Monmon Akter

F4PRINT

**Published by
F4P Publishing Group
P.O. Box 280742
Nashville, TN 37228
https://f4printinc.com**

Copyright © 2024 by Sabrina Phillips Evans
Evang8sabrina@gmail.com

Description:
A message from Grandma-Ma to Grandchildren and Great-grandchildren.

All rights reserved.
No part of this book may be reproduced in any form including by electronic or mechanical means without permission in writing from the author, except by a reviewer who may quote brief passages in a review.

ISBN: 978-1736553-26-8
Printed in the United States of America – First Printing

Thank you for your support.

Dedication

God has blessed my husband Glenn and me with 9 beautiful grandchildren and 4 great-grands. We love all of you dearly, and our prayer is that you will grow strong in faith, love, and have a relationship with
Jesus Christ.

Some of you call me Grandma, one calls me Grandma-Brie, but four of you call me Ma-ma-ma or Grandma-ma, and I call you my little ones.

Kaylee, Samuel, MaKenzie, and Nathan Jr.

Your cousins, my great-grands, are right on your heels, and with that being said, I dedicate this book to you, and the little ones coming behind you, with much love.

My dear little ones, you're not so little anymore.
You're growing up and getting bigger every day.
Oh, how I miss holding your little bodies in my arms,
while looking at your beautiful faces, listening to you
cry, watching you turn over, crawl, and, of course,
taking your first step.

Have I told you just how important you are to me?
Well, let me tell you, I love you so much.
So much it cannot be measured, which means
my love for you will never end.

Like God's love is for mankind, it never ends. John 3:16 says, "For God so loved the world that he gave His only son Jesus and whoever believes in him will have everlasting life!" You see, little ones, you are very special not only to me but to your parents, grandparents, aunties, uncles, cousins, and family, near and far who are concerned about your well-being.

However, the greatest love is the love God has for us all! In His love we have peace, joy, wisdom, strength, discipline, and so much more. That's why we pray to Him. I am sure your parents have taught you how to do that. As Grandpa would say, "Talk to God", and may I add, you can talk to God about anything.

Now that you are school-age I am sure you have much to share about your teachers, meeting new friends, and all the wonderful things you experience from learning. You are my bravest little ones. I am so proud that you're doing well in reading, writing, and making me those lovely pictures that I place on my fridge. All of you have beautiful gifts and talents lingering inside of you to be great leaders, so dream big, but remember the greatest leaders are honest, truthful, humble, thankful, and hard workers.

One day you'll achieve goals on your own. However, right now I will settle for good children who do their homework and clean their rooms. Look how you have blossomed like flowers in the spring, full of energy, smiles, and wonder! So while you are spending our money keep filling those piggy banks, and we will teach you to save and spend your money wisely.

Remember to "Listen and Obey" because all of you have much to learn. Kaylee, Samuel, Mackenzie, and Nathan Jr., love one another, be kind to each other. Kay, you have two other brothers, Alex and Marley. Be that loving sister. My hope and dream is to see each of you grands and great-grands grow up, graduate, and be the best "you" you can be. Make a difference in this world, love yourself, so you can help somebody else. Show kindness, determination, and resilience. Watch out for hurts along the way, they are sure to come.

Yes, some are more painful than others, like skinning your knee or maybe getting spanked for disobeying, even betrayal by a friend or bullying. But you are not alone, we all have experienced pain and discipline. Change is a part of life. What I want you to know is this: Never be afraid to talk about it. Don't keep secrets that make you feel guilty or ashamed, even if it's your fault. Always remember you are loved and that Jesus, God's son, gave His life for us, so we could be forgiven of our sins. We've all done wrong and made mistakes, believe me!

Predators lurk around us, especially on those cell phones and computers. Be careful, always talk to your parents about any unknown callers or texts because the older you get the more watchful you must be at school, parks, stores, restaurants, and home. Never ever open the door without permission.

Pay Attention! Look around you. What would you do if there was a fire? Have you thought about it? And, of course, you know how to call 911, right?

I love you guys especially when you call or text me. I'm only a phone call away and will come right over. When we eat and play together, my ears are always open to what you have to say. You make my heart so glad. (*Smile*)
You guys make my day!

Before you close the book, I have to remind you of something, and you must remind yourself every day of the same. What I want you to do is make declarations... Oh, what is that you ask?

Well, declarations means what you say about yourself, to declare who you really are. You are more than just your parents' child. You are God's Creation!

Say to yourself:

I am smart, intelligent, strong, beautiful, and thankful. I do my best at home, school, and in my activities. I will treat others as I would like to be treated, with kindness, respect, and truth. I am not a bully, and I will not be bullied.

I am grateful for all my blessings, my parents, my family, my friends. I may fail, but I am not a failure. I am special and successful because "I can do all things through Christ who gives me strength." My mind and body are precious, so I will take care of them. I will think right and eat right. I will grow up to be the best me I can be.

        I love God, I love me, and I love others!

Readability Score

Easy to Read

Reader's Age: 8 - 12 (Grades 3 - 6)

Other Books by the Author

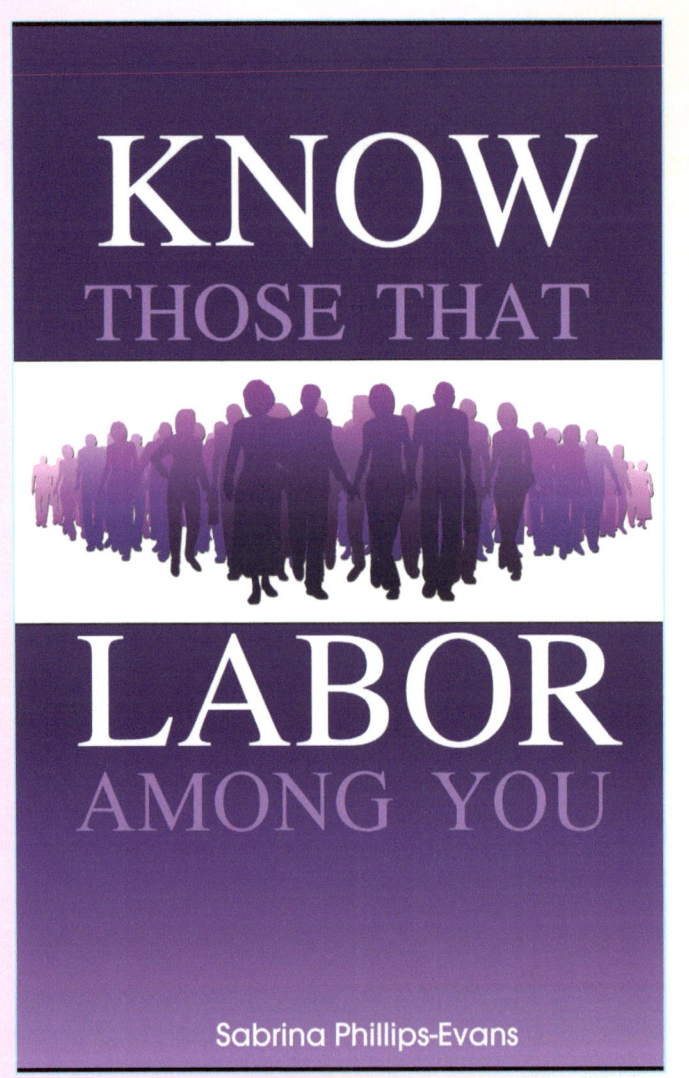

All titles are available on Amazon.

www.ingramcontent.com/pod-product-compliance
Lightning Source LLC
Chambersburg PA
CBHW041526070526
44585CB00002B/106